MY COLOURING
IN PROJECTS
FOR MERCHANDISING
ON
PRINT ON DEMAND
WEBSITES

By
Richard
Gallacher

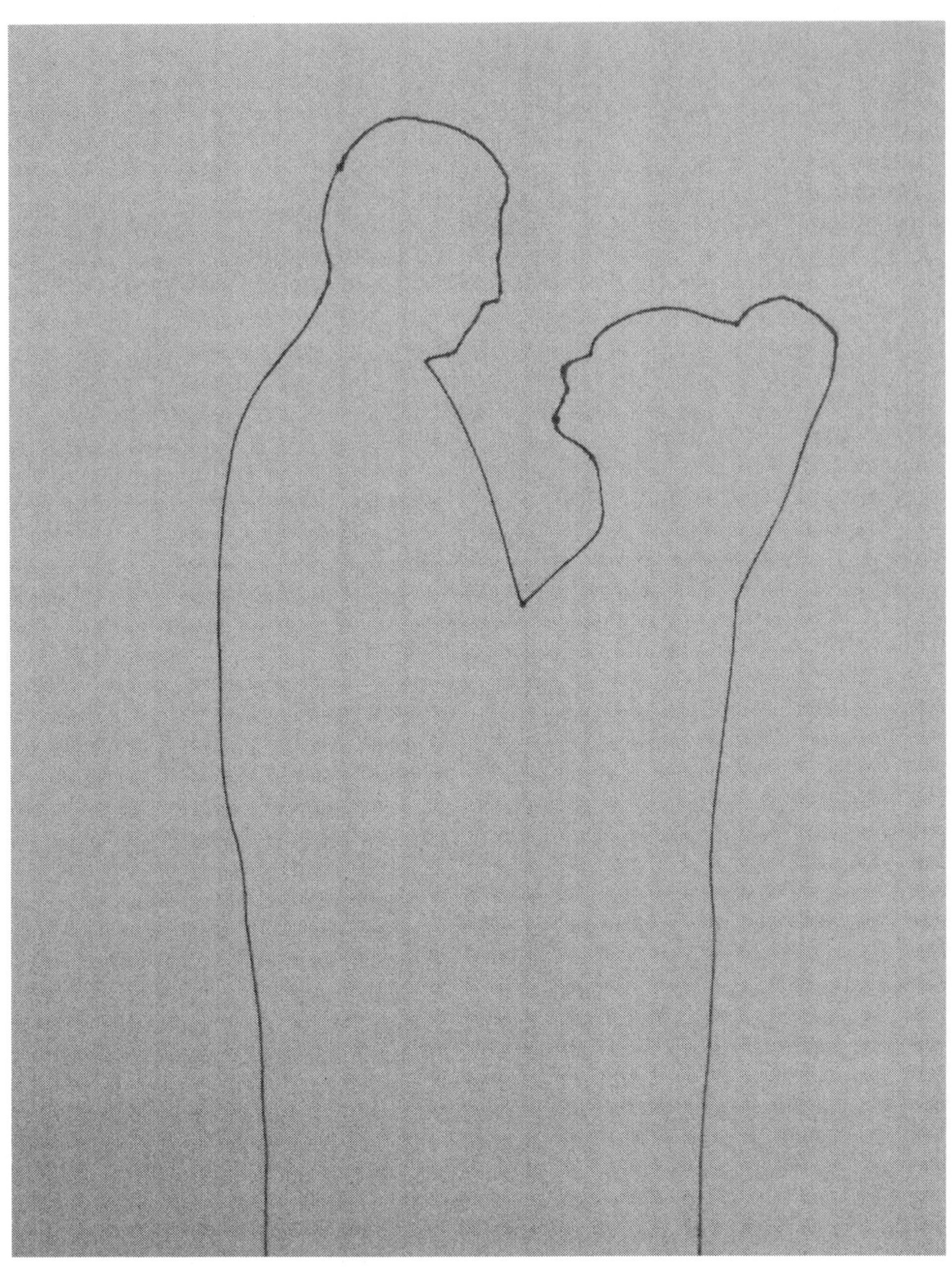

The lovers , add your version of
the lovers fill in the blank , colour
it in , dress them in the fashion of
your choice.

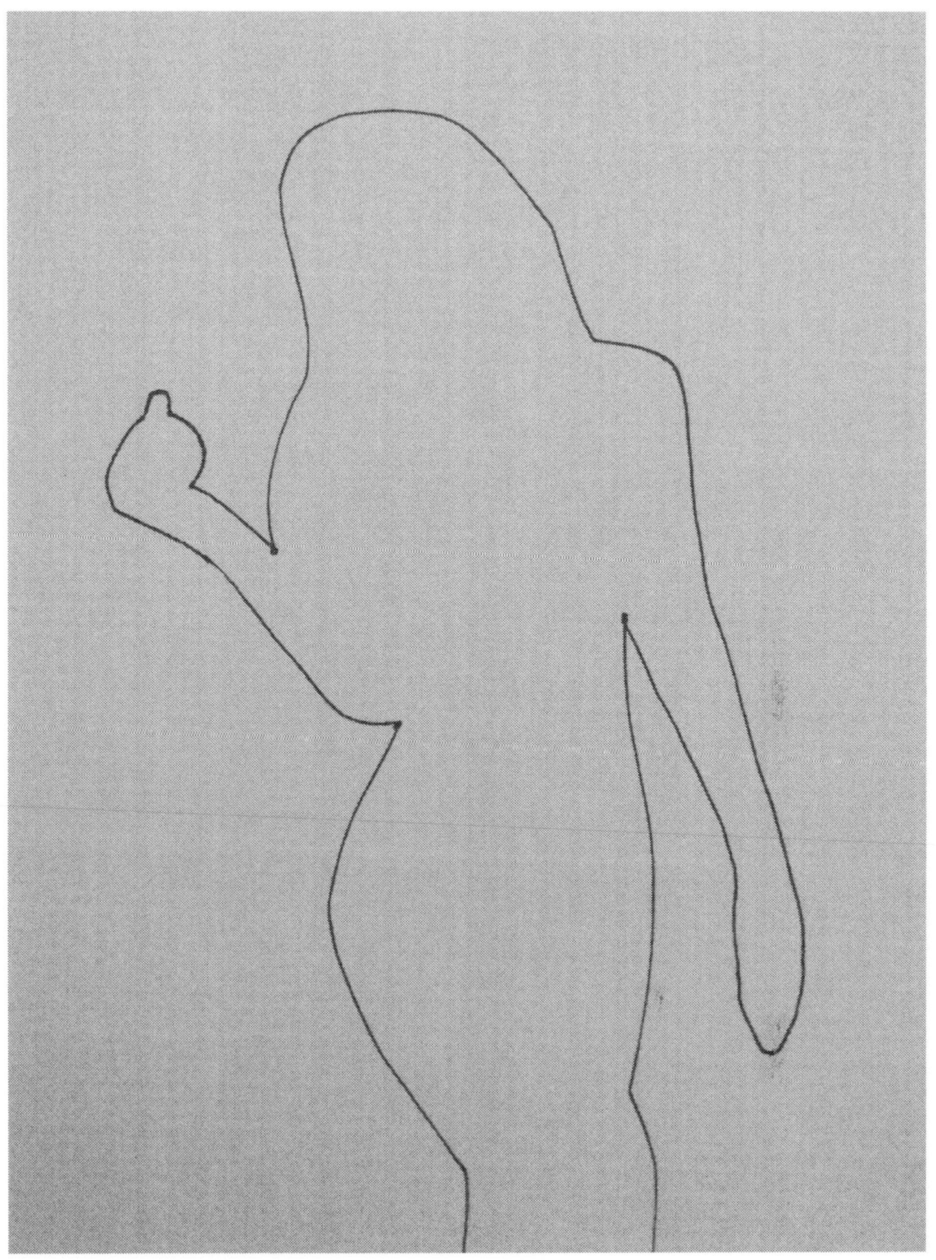

The beautiful young woman
stands gazing at an object in her
hand , fill in the blank , colour it
in , choose object and fashion.

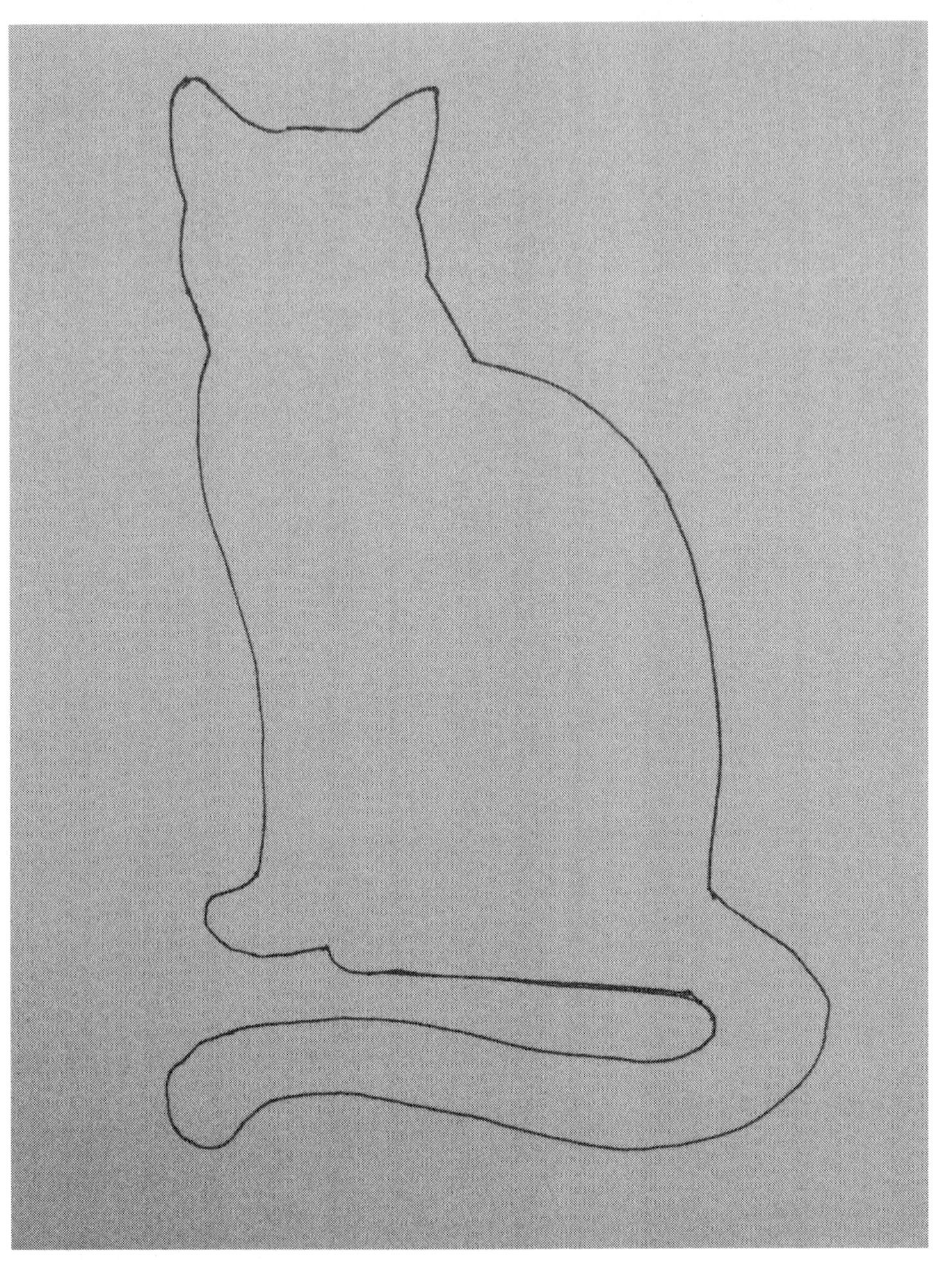

Colour your Cat , let your artistic juices flow , photograph your image or copy file and upload to print on demand site.

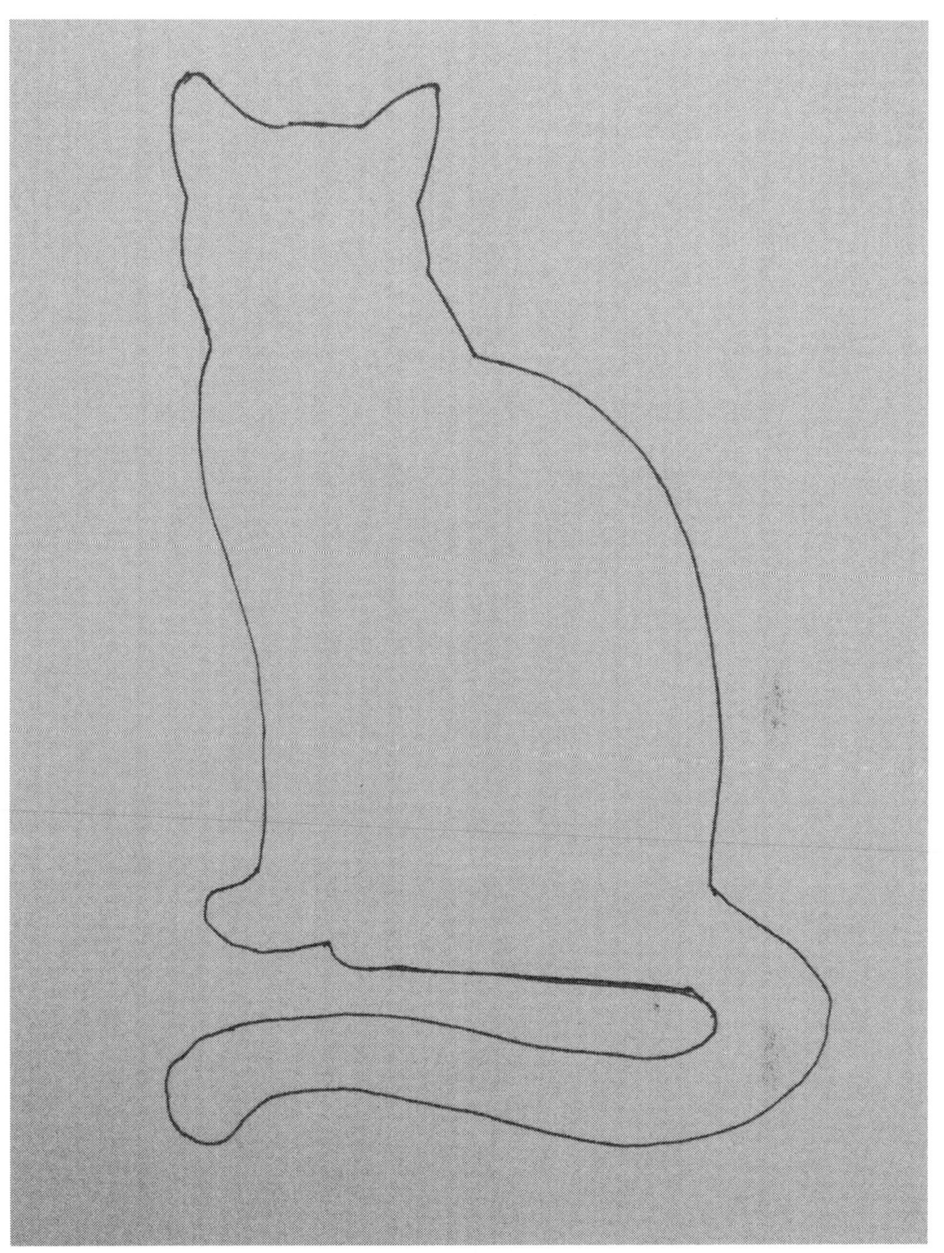

Now do another one totally different , upload to on demand merchandising platform.

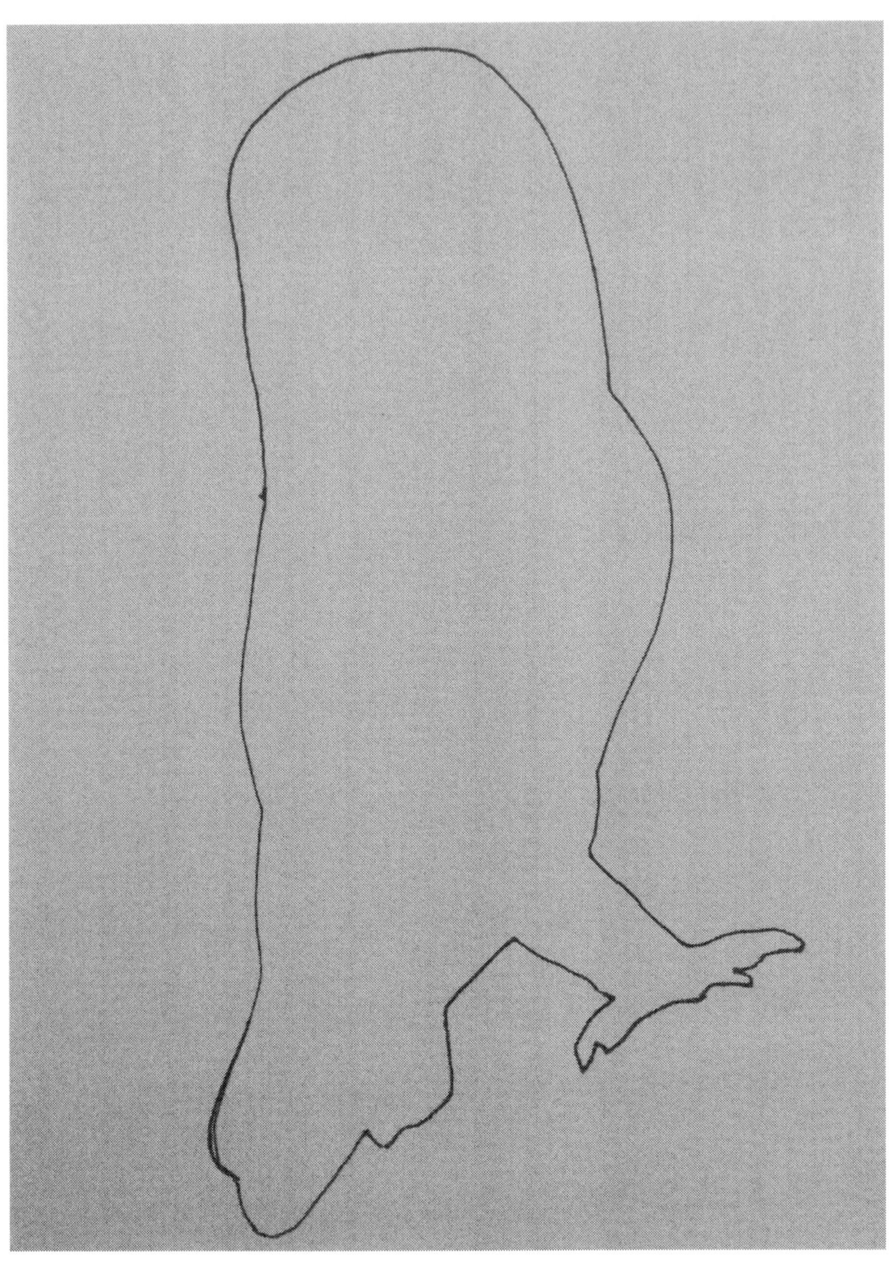

The wise Owl choose your
colours and style make it totally
unique in design to yourself.

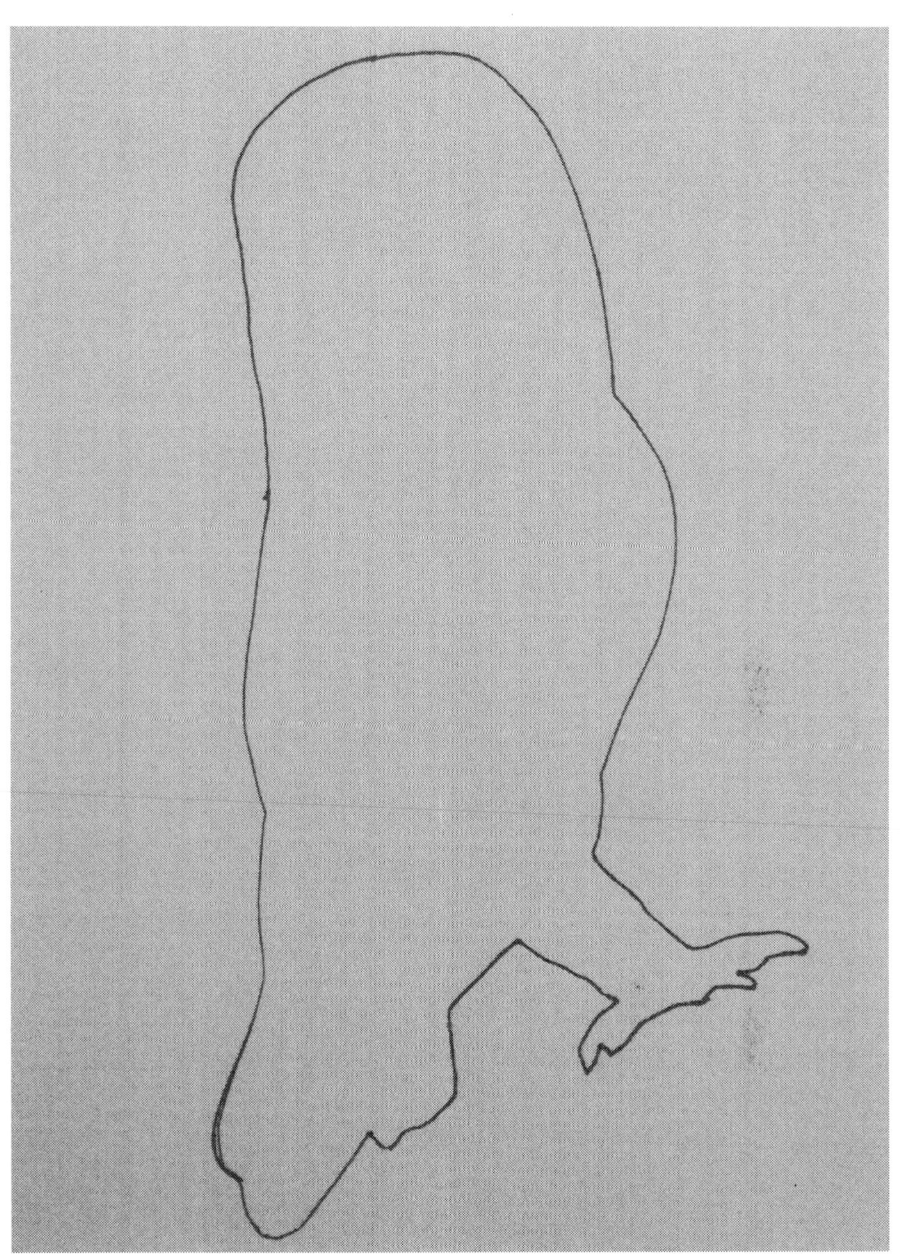

Again make it totally unique to
your design , maybe add a branch
of a tree , for it to grip , have fun.

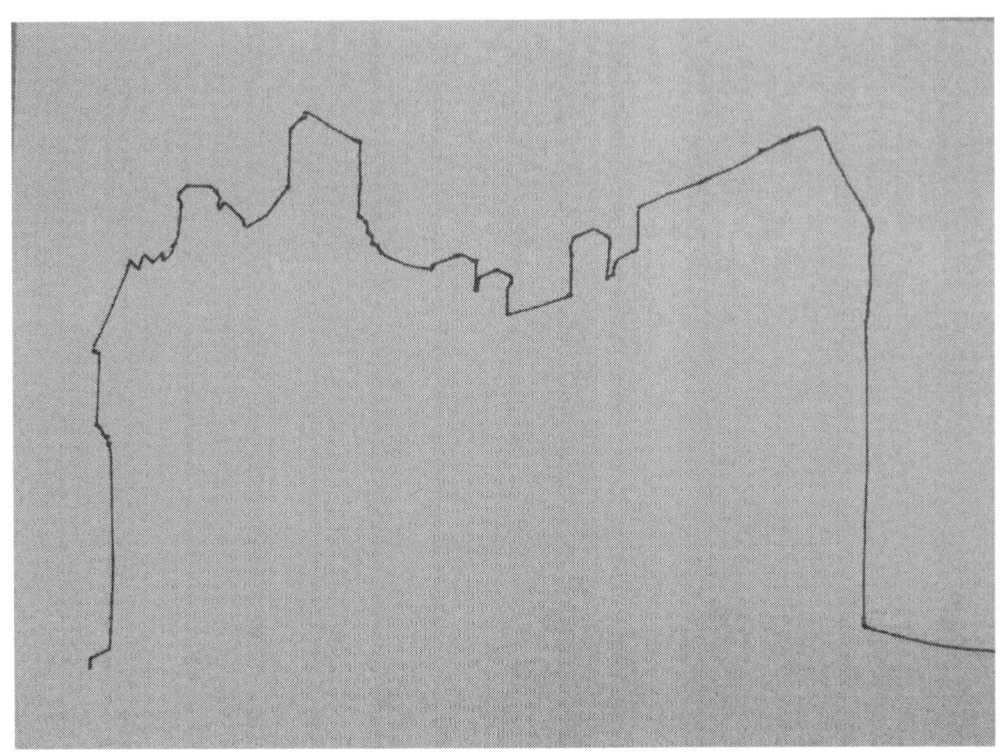

The castle , add brick
work windows , choose
old or modern
architecture make your
design totally original
then sell.

The castle , add brick
work windows , choose
old or modern
architecture make your
design totally original
then sell. Choose your
colours let your
imagination run wild
and free.

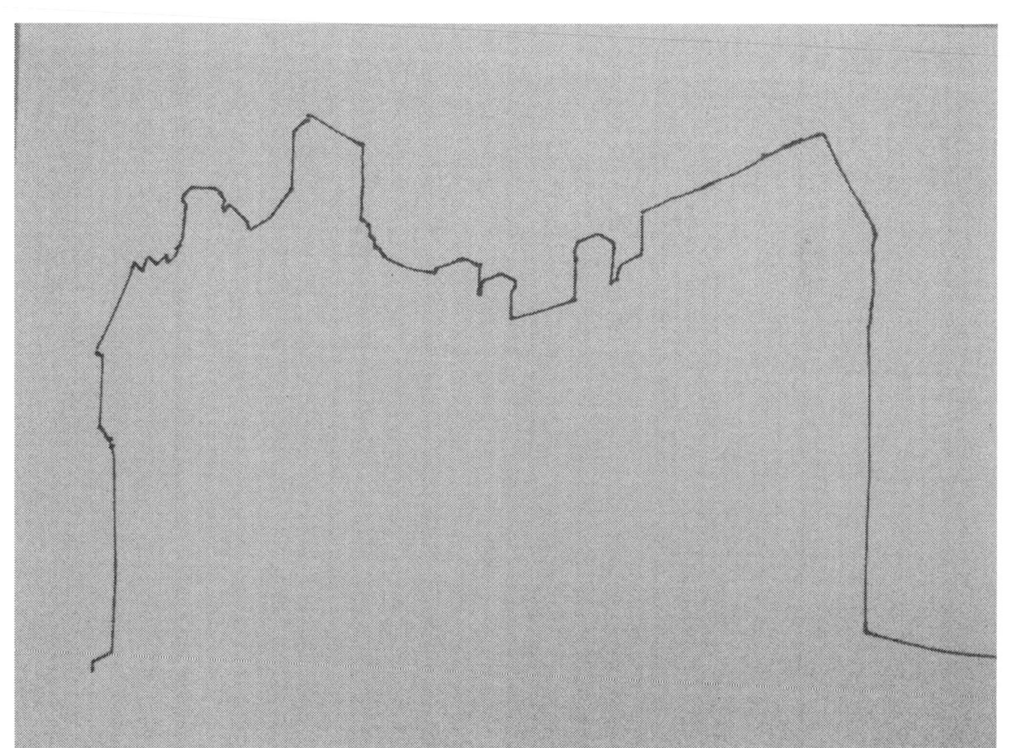

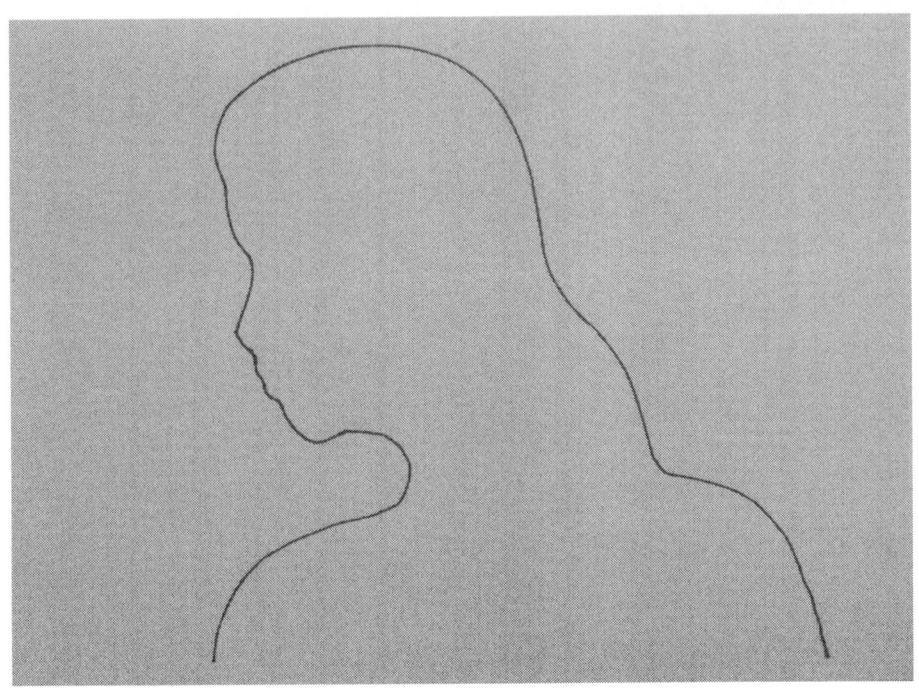

The Beautiful young
woman , which colour
of hair will you give her
the choice is up to you ,
be original with your
design be free.

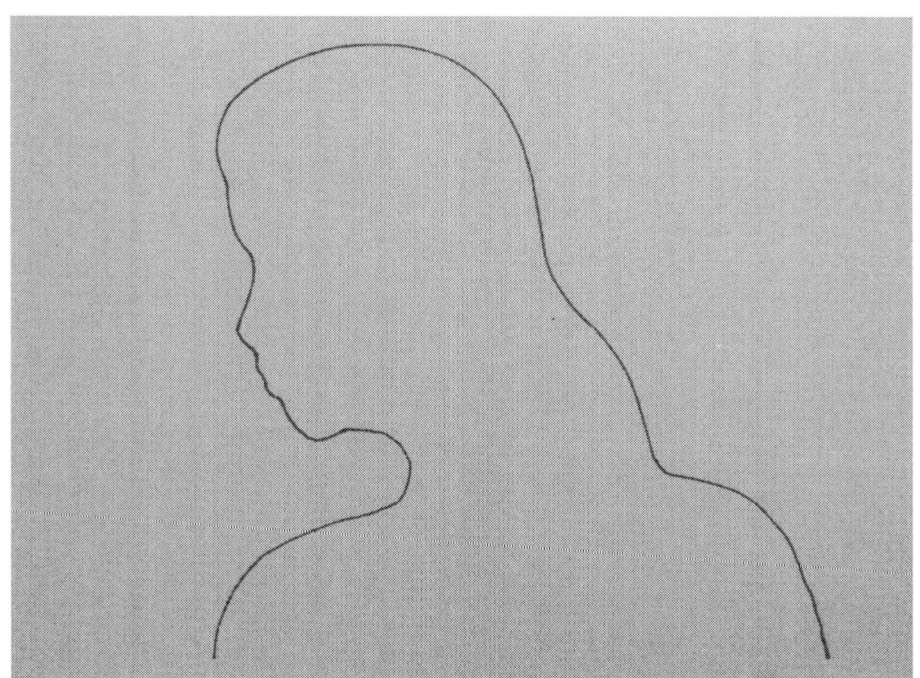

Will she have blonde hair , black hair , red hair , the list is almost endless and the artistic freedom is yours.

The wild stag of
Scotland , is he looking
at you , or looking away
from you , it's up to you
, what is he looking at ,
a Loch and mountains
perhaps , you decide.

If the stag looked at
you maybe this one
could look at the Loch
and mountains , the
choice is yours.

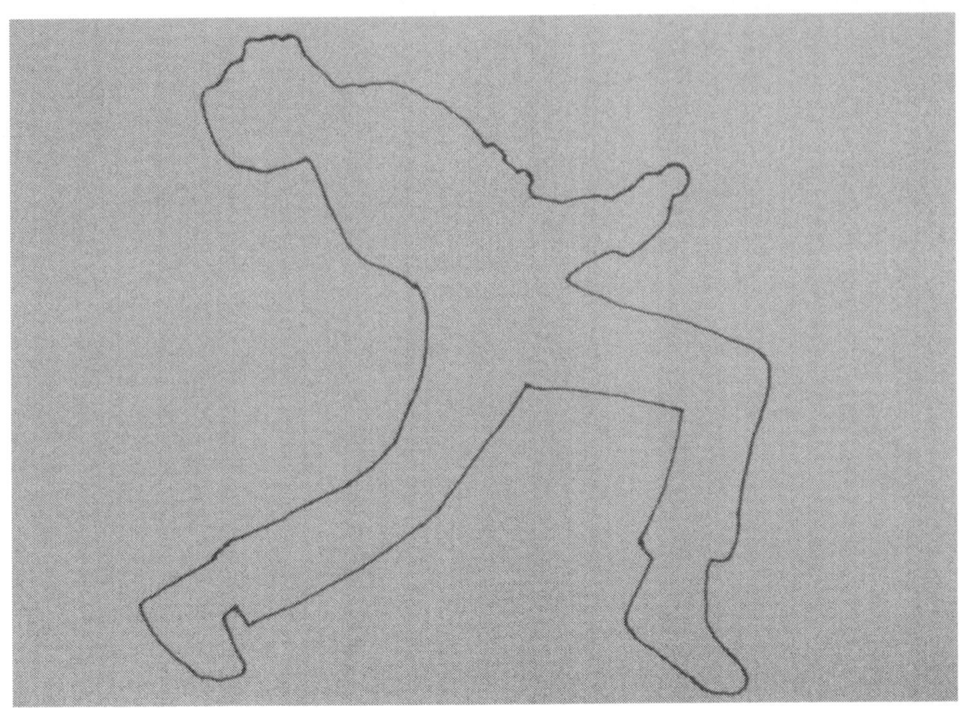

Here is one of the greatest men ever to have lived , Freddie Mercury a songwriting genius a performer and musician of a truly iconic status.

I personally feel that in the case of this publication and as tribute I will add four images for you to colour how ever you like.

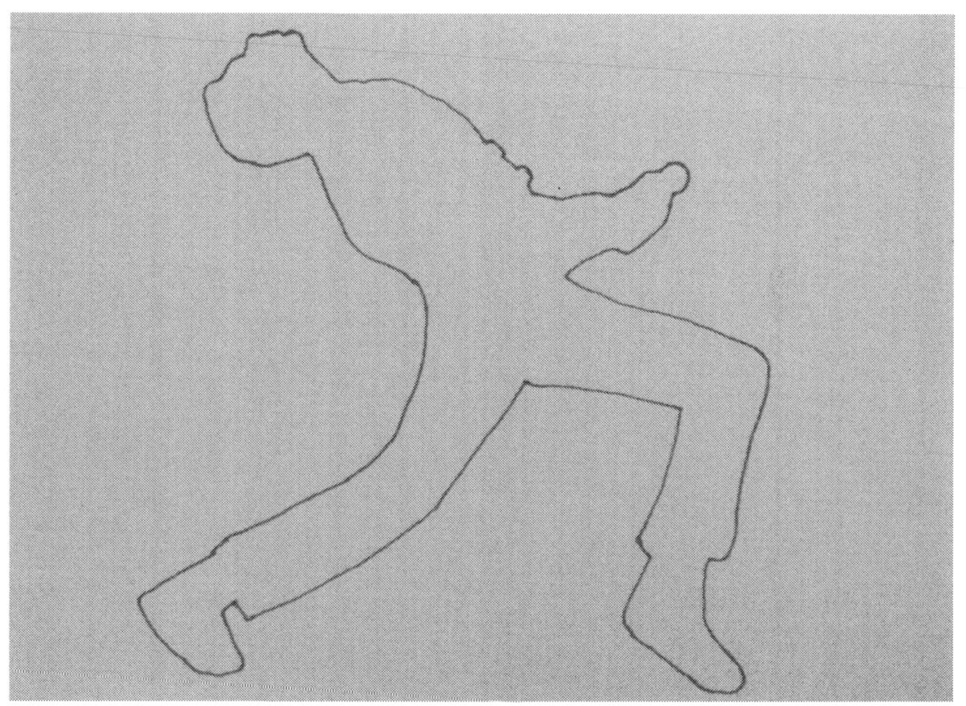

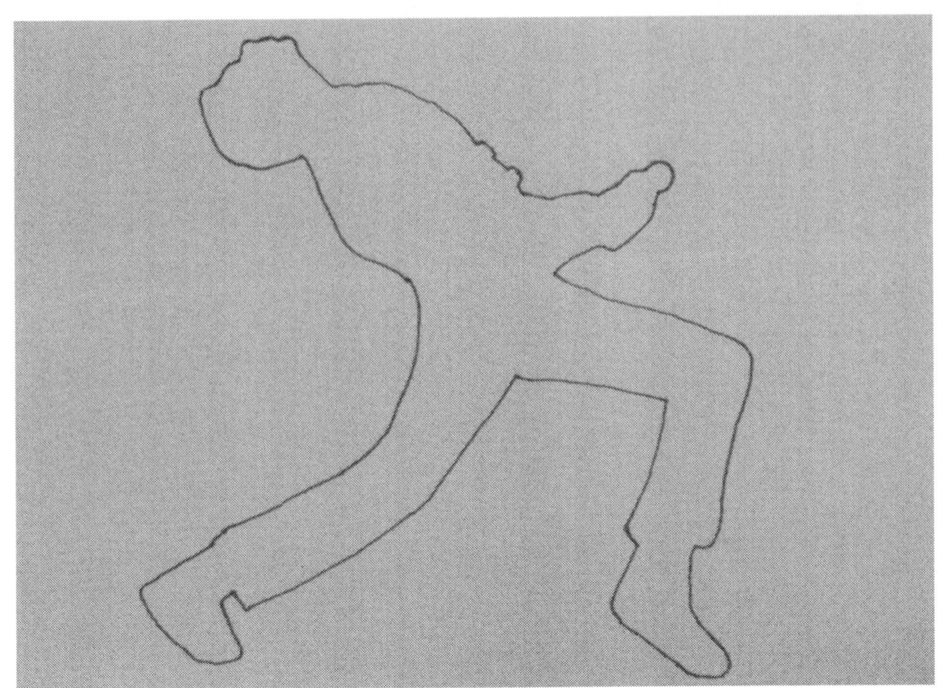

For a treat if you have never heard of Freddie Mercury , go on to YouTube and watch Freddie Mercury versus the crowd , you will love it , and it may inspire your colouring in.

Use your imagination
and experiment with
different outfits , then
add them to on
demand sites and
merchandise your
creation.

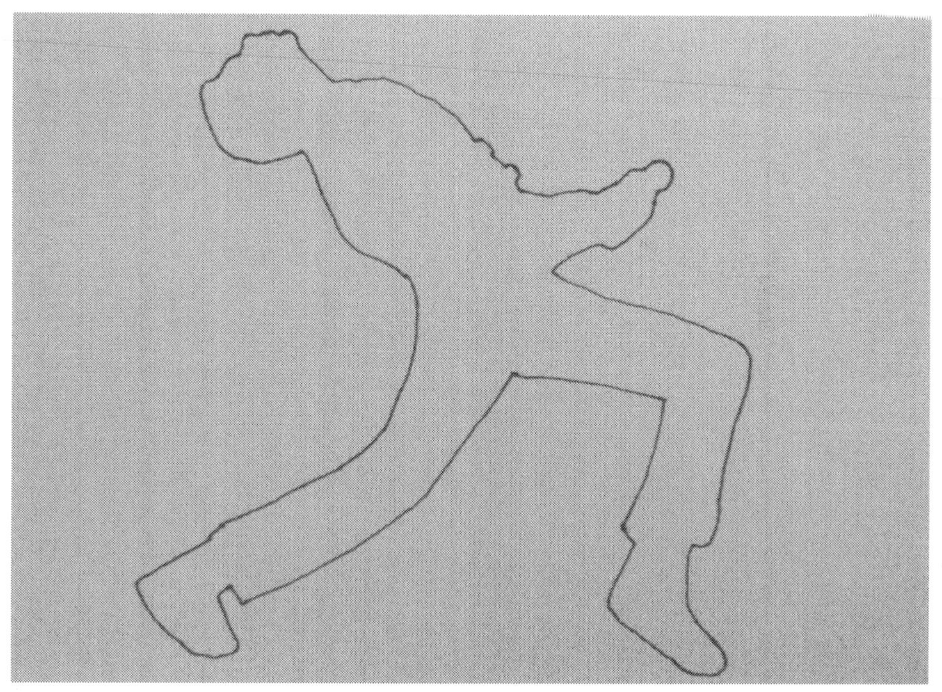

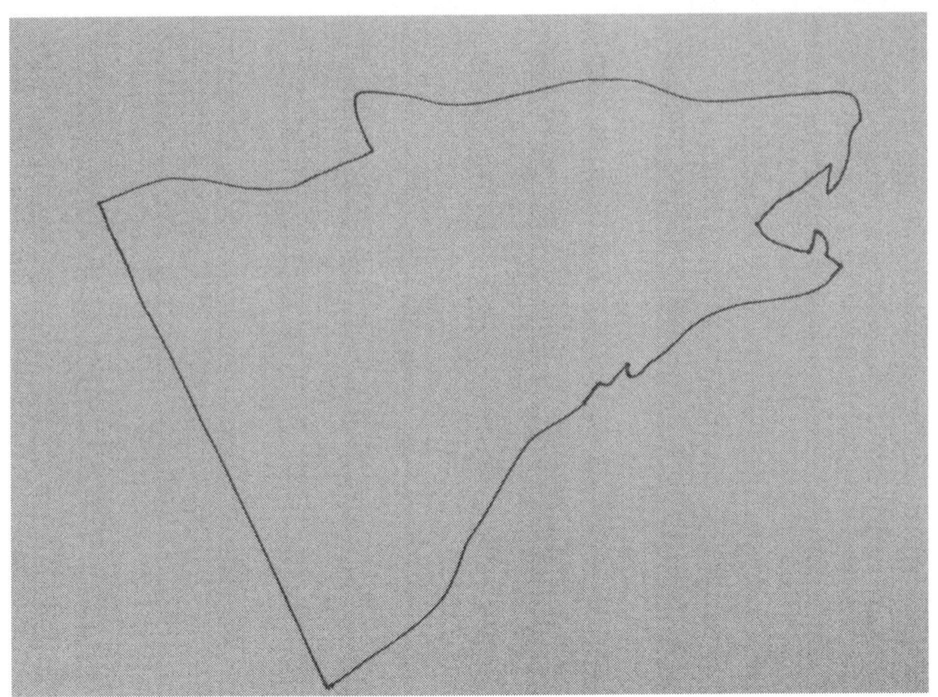

The wolf howling colour
as you like , maybe he
is a grey wolf , maybe
he is black or white ,
you decide.

Remember google search print on demand sites for your art works once you have completed the book , upload files or photos.

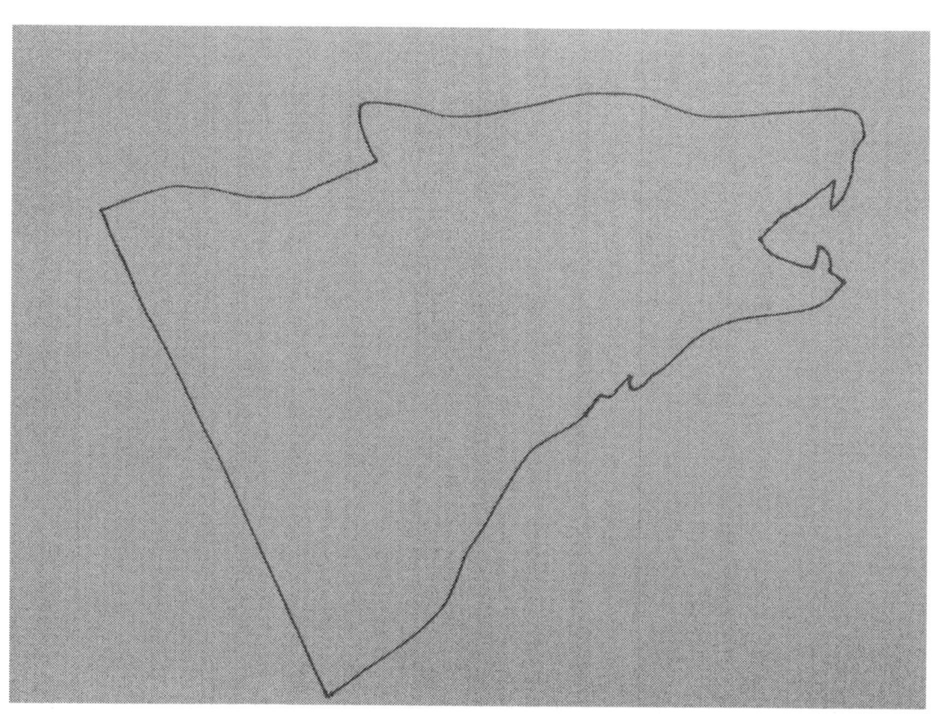

The singer songwriter ,
choose to fill in the
blank with guitar and
his clothes , you choose
guitar and outfit , have
fun.

Where is he sitting , on
a fallen tree , a rock by
the beach , the choice
is yours , have fun.

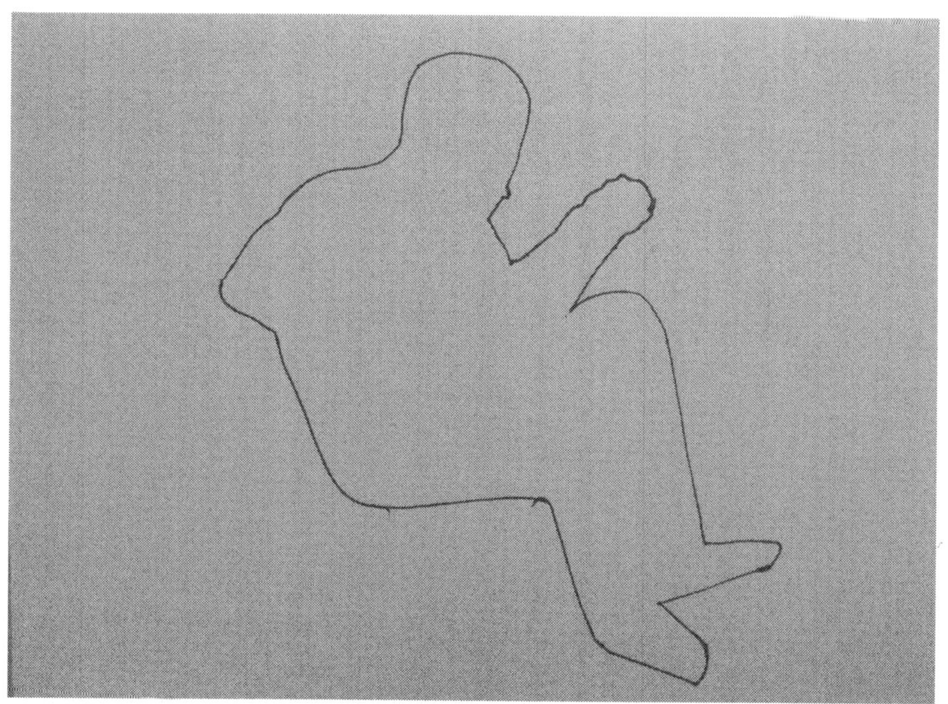

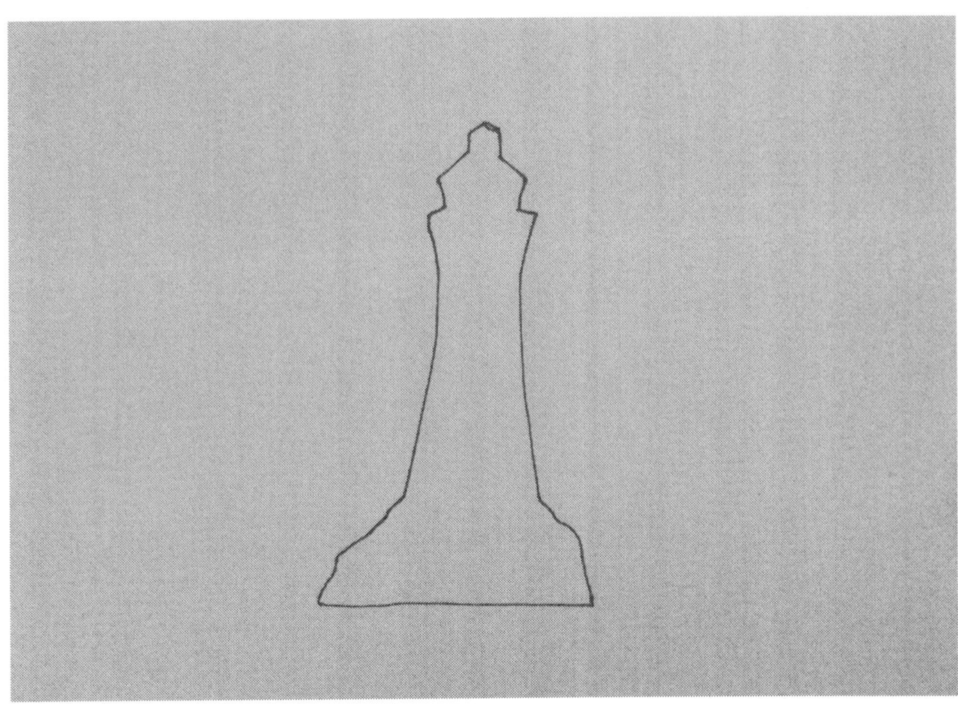

The lighthouse , is it set in the middle of the water or at the lands end , you decide , have fun.

The beautiful dolphin ,
which colour will you
choose , blu , grey , a
mixture of both , a
rainbow the choice is
yours have fun.

Now here is the
beautiful unicorn I will
be placing four unicorn
images in total for you
to let your creative
juices flow.

I hope you really
enjoyed colouring in
and bringing your
unicorns to life.

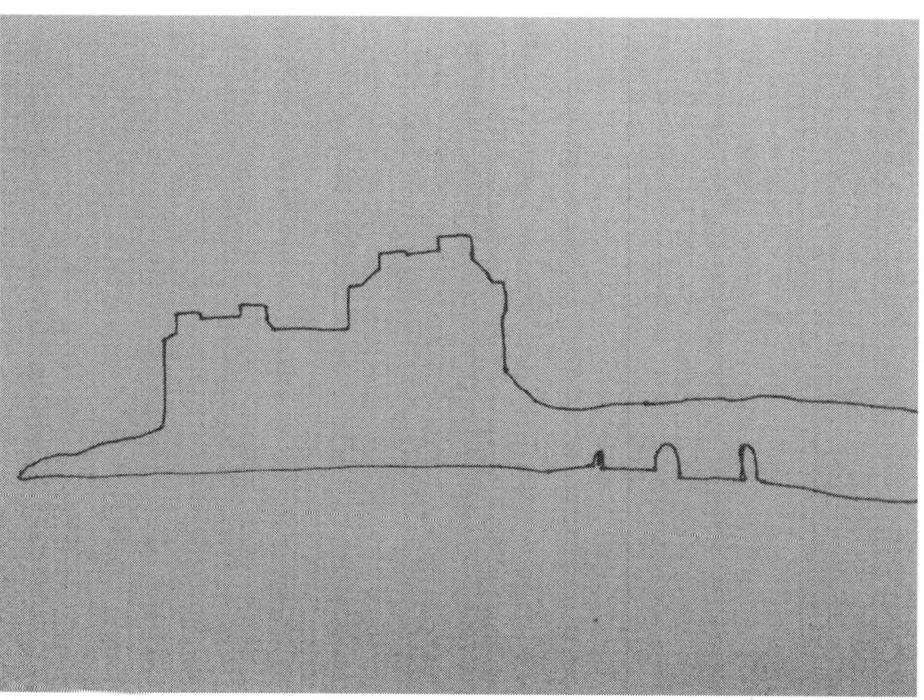

This is Eilean Donan castle in Scotland , probably most famous for the film Highlander starring Christopher Lambert and Sir Sean Connery to name but a few ,

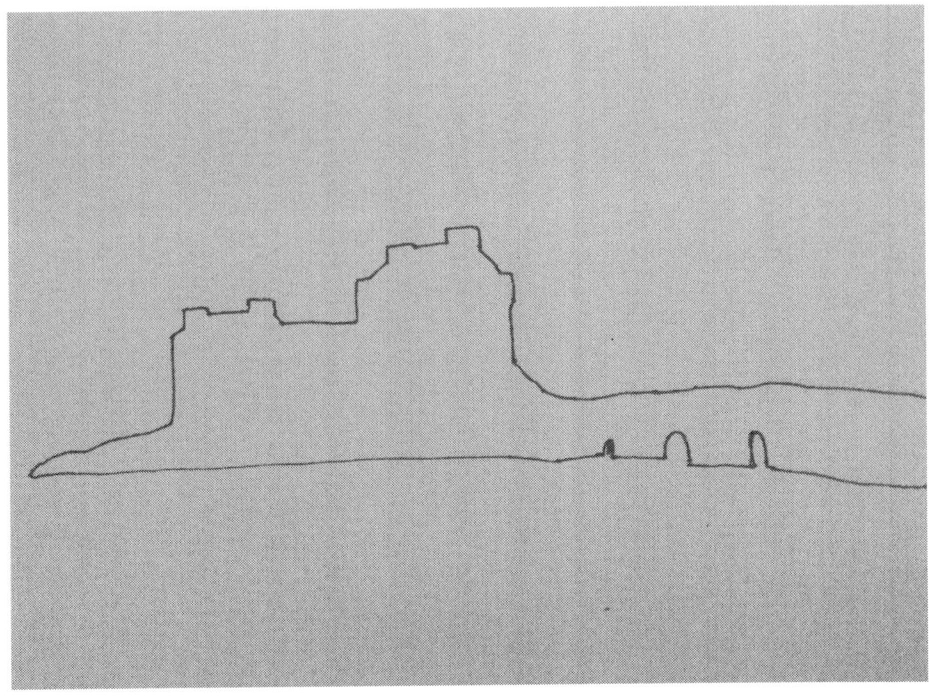

Again like the other
castle earlier on in the
publication , fill in the
blank , is it old is it
modern it is up to you ,
have fun.

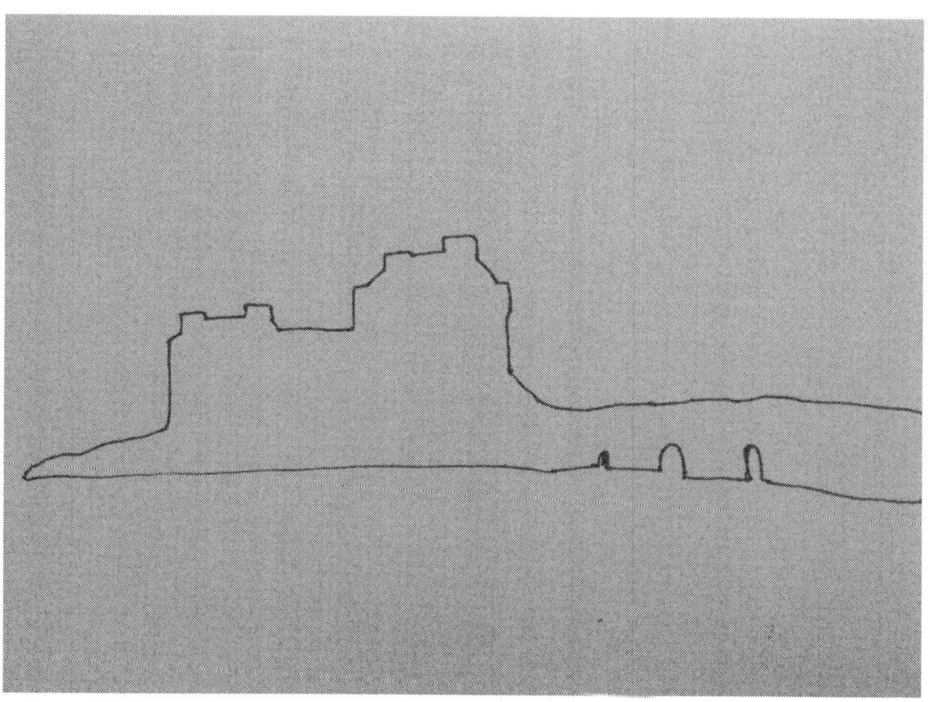

Is the artwork set in the
day time , night time ,
summer , winter it is
once more up to you ,
have fun.

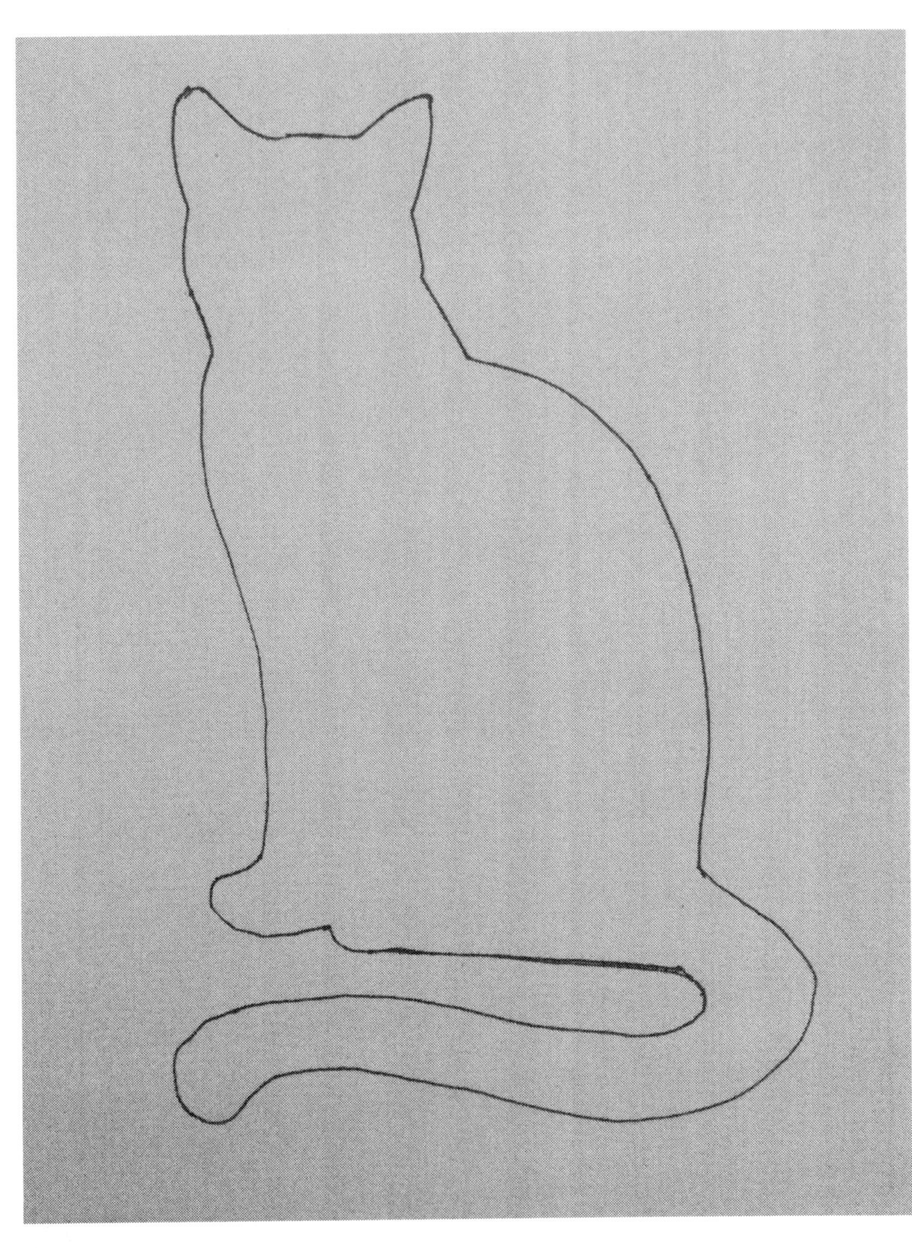

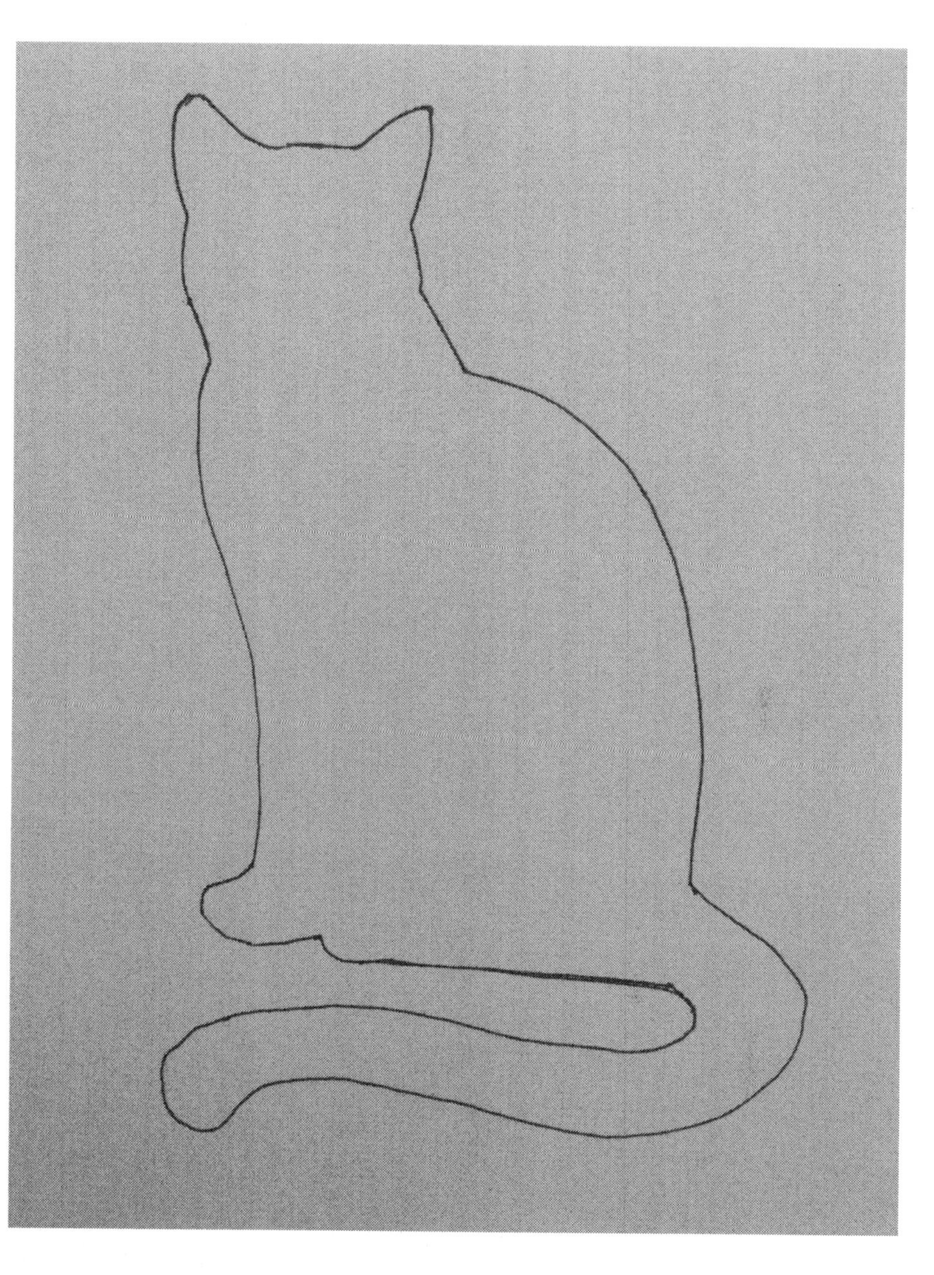

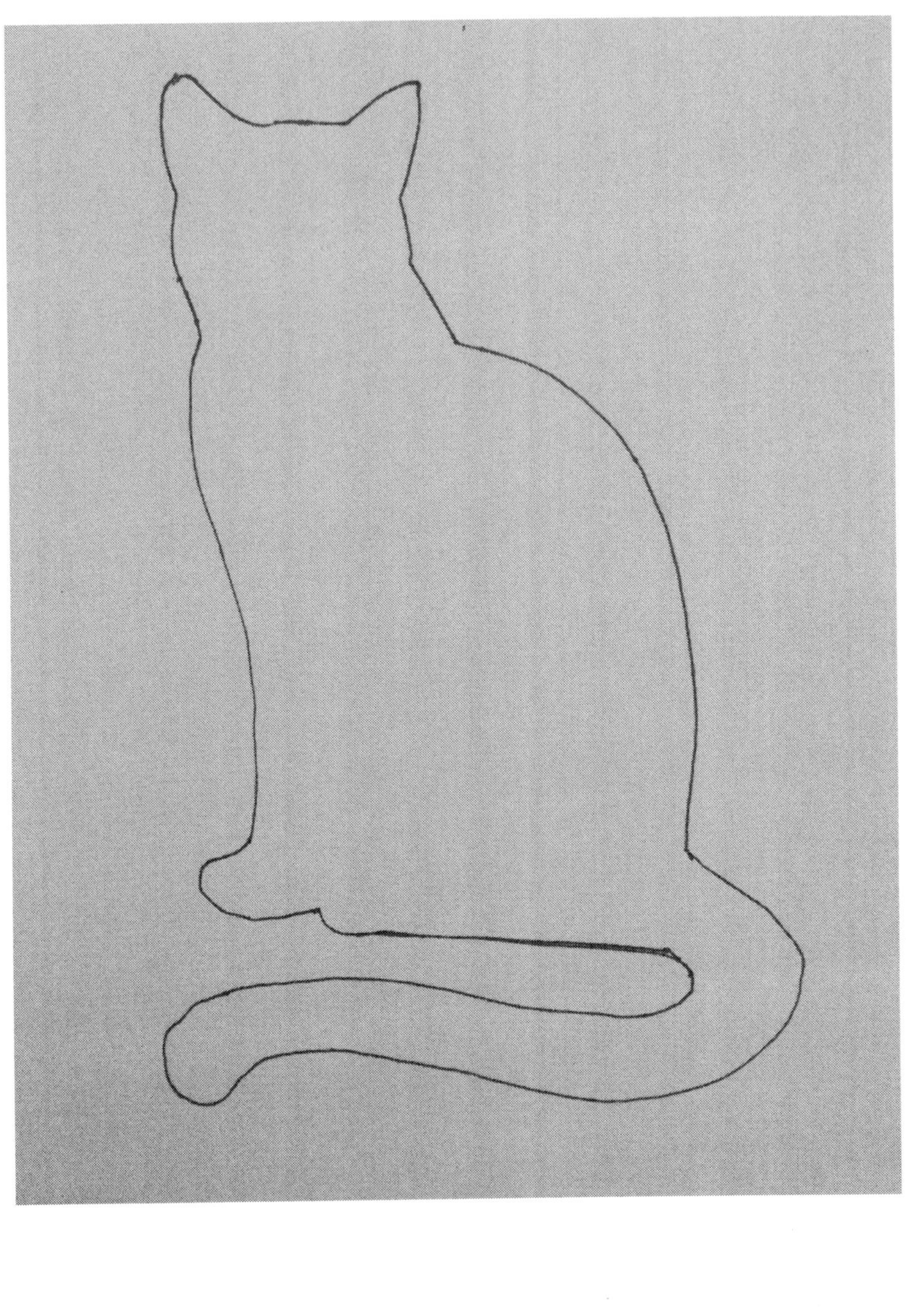

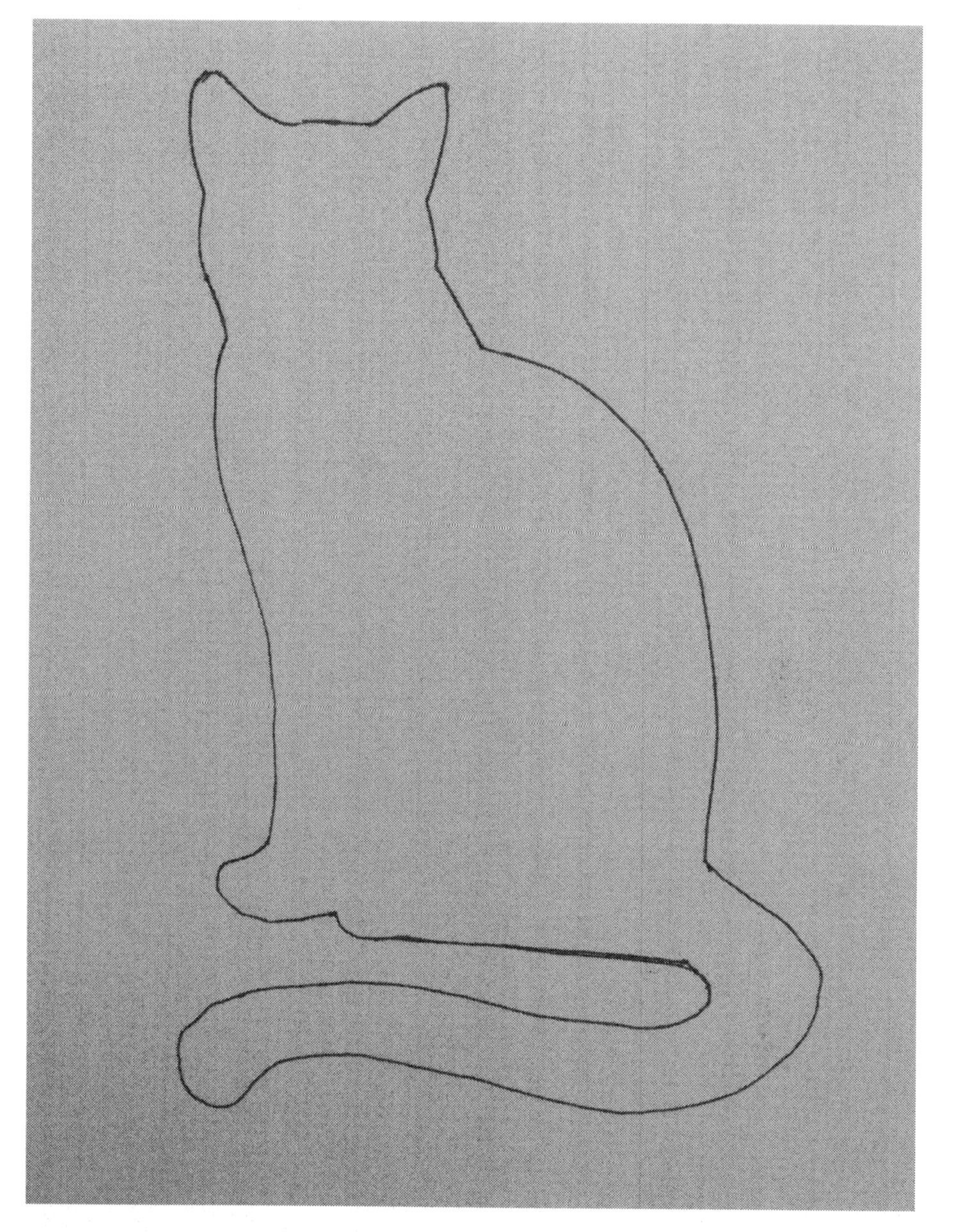

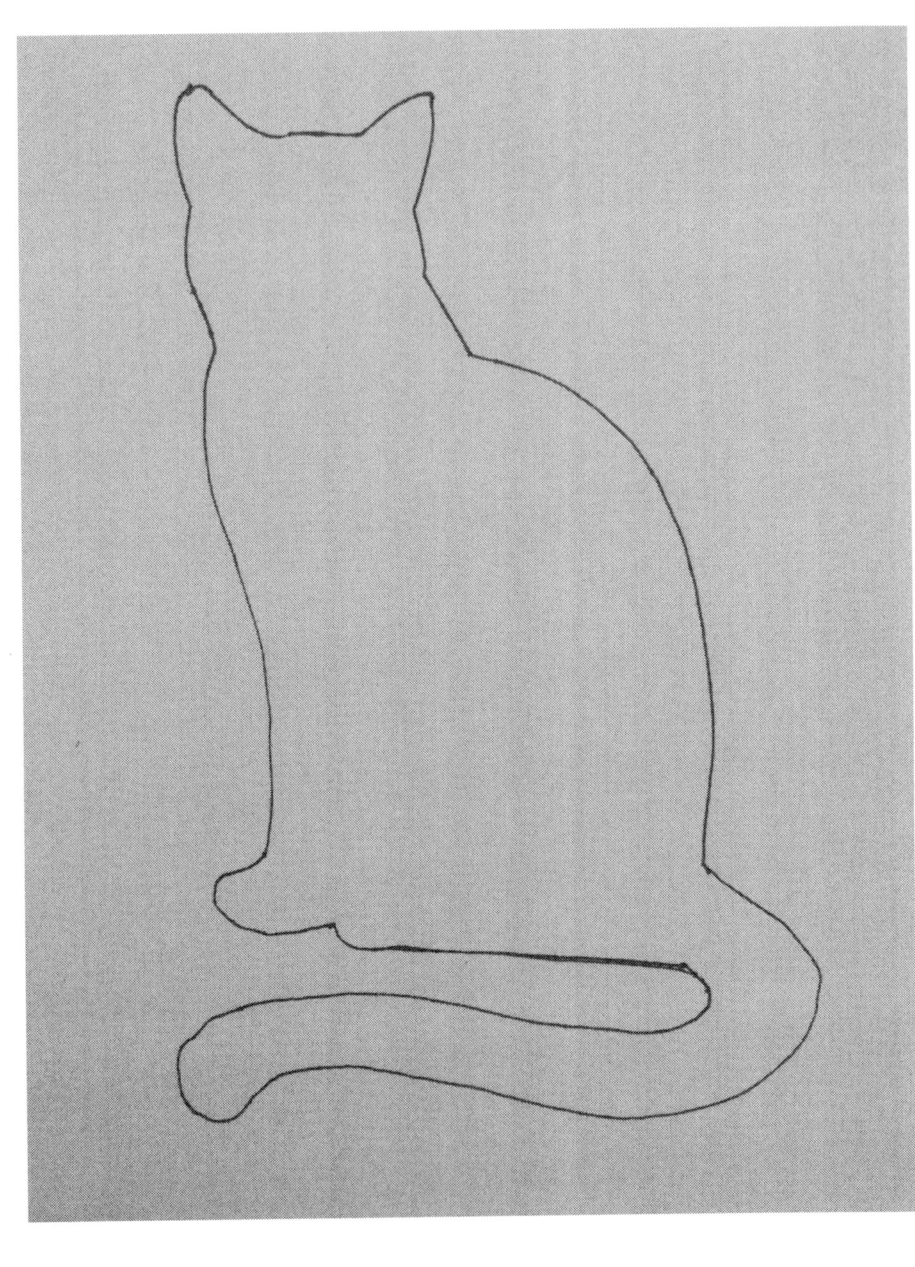

I have decided to finish
the publication with
five blank cat images
for you to fill in and
colour , for best results
when using this book to
colour place card under
the image you are
working on and use
colouring in pencils.
Have fun.

Printed in Great Britain
by Amazon